ANDREW MARTIN

INTERNATIONAL
INTERIOR DESIGN
REVIEW

VOLUME 3

MARTIN WALLER • SARAH STEWART-SMITH

ANDREW MARTIN
INTERNATIONAL

EDITOR: MARTIN WALLER
TEXT: SARAH STEWART-SMITH
PROJECT EXECUTIVE: JACQUELINE WILLERS
PRODUCT DESIGN: GRAPHICOM EXPRESS

First Published in 1999 by

ANDREW MARTIN
INTERNATIONAL

ISBN 1840910348

Reproduction by Yale Press. Printed by Grupo Mondadori.

ACKNOWLEDGMENTS

The author and publisher wish to thank all the owners and designers of the projects
featured in this book.

They also thank the following photographers :

Jason Lowe, Caroline Gavazzi, Henry Wilson, Gilles Trillard, Felix Adilson,
Fritz von der Schulenburg, Frances Janisch, John Stoddart, Betsy Cherry, Chris Gascoigne,
Andreas von Einsiedel, Peo Eriksson, Magnus Anesund, Joy von Tiedmann, Peter Seller,
Paul Redmond, Ray Main, Ken Kirkwood, Peter Aprahamian, Klaus Frahm,
Etchika Werner Studio, Mary Nicols, William Cummings (front cover), Neil Ferrin, Paul Tang,
Yuri Ridyakin, Ken Hayden, Yavuz Draman, Mehmet Mutaf, Jose Miquel Figueiredo,
Scott Frances, Roger Spencer-Jones, Joseph Sy, Facundo de Zuviria, Francki Burger,
Ake E:Son Lindman, Anders Hage, Mark Luscombe-Whyte, The Conde Nast Publications -
House & Garden, Bill Lafevor, Bob Marchant, Alex Rogers, Gal Oppido, Eduardo Girao, Beto
Riginik, David Glomb, Gordan Beall, David Bache, Tim Clinch, Jan Holden, B. Cunningham.

Distributed by Conran Octopus Limited, 2-4 Heron Quays, London E14 4JP.

conran
OCTOPUS

INTRODUCTION

At Andrew Martin we are very proud to organize the International Interior Designer of the Year Award. In just a few years, it has become acknowledged as the Oscars of the interiors world.

Already the winners of the title constitute a pretty distinguished bunch - Kelly Hoppen in 1996, Thomas Pheasant in 1997 and Michael Reeves in 1998 - but as significant has been the extraordinary breadth of work submitted for the award and this review includes some of the best entries from around the world. You can see for yourself how difficult the task of judging the competition is. Comparing Hong Kong's Mandarin Hotel with a South African beach house, a London attic flat with a Las Vegas mansion. We have been lucky enough to have some impressive people on our judging panel who have been brave enough to stick their necks out and make firm decisions. Amongst them have been Anouska Hempel, Alexandra Schulman, David Tang, Joseph Ettedgui, Jo Malone and A.A Gill.

Interior design has been with us throughout the second millennium. At its start the Islamic world was pre-eminent with its fabulous work still visible in Andalucia and Istanbul. As the renaissance rolled back the dark ages, the treasures of Rome, Venice and Florence were being designed. Louis XIV in 17th century France was perhaps the greatest ever patron of interior design. By the time we reached the end of the 18th century, interior design had reached such a pinnacle of achievement and sophistication that we still revere it as a golden age. Its principal figures like Adam and Chippendale are still household names today in a way that no current designer or architect can emulate. However what has set the 20th century apart, especially the last 25 years, is the extraordinary widening of interest in the whole subject of design. Everybody has a view on chintz versus minimalism, Liaigre versus Linley.

This is a worldwide phenomenon. But people in different parts of the world have different perspectives. Taste in India is utterly different from taste in Japan, not better or worse, just different. The cool tradition of Swedish design much admired in London is not a hit in the Gulf. Different countries and different climates ensure different design viewpoints.

What this book tries to show is how the world's leading designers wrestle with these different viewpoints as they endeavour to develop the boundaries of interior design. The fascination is in how many solutions there are to the same design puzzle.   MARTIN WALLER

Michael Reeves

Designer: Michael Reeves. **Country:** United Kingdom. **Style:** Mixing looks. I can see any space as it should be, however small or large. **Work:** Mainly private houses - between ten and 20 at a time. **Favourite colours:** The range of taupe from the palest ivory to chocolate brown. However, I love to use aqua blues and greens, and to add hot pink, lavender or red as a highlight. **Vital element:** Space, comfort and great lighting. **Must have:** The most comfortable bed that your budget can stand, plus all the electrical gadgets that make life easy. **Object of desire:** A New York penthouse apartment. **Most inspiring buildings:** Dakota and Chrysler buildings in New York - they are astounding. **Admired designers:** Sally Sirkin Lewis, who founded the fabric company, J Robert Scott, the interior designer, Jonathan Reed and I love Saladino's work. **Good shopping:** My own shop and I am particularly passionate about Takashimaya in New York. They have the best eclectic mix of everything. **Best buy:** An enormous Dutch portrait. **Pet hates:** Festoon blinds, 'itsy-bitsy' styling, overuse of fabric at windows, artificial flowers, glossy bathroom tiles and also patterned china and house plants.

Reeves' minimalism: strong architecture softened by witty artefacts and clever lighting.

'We have reached the point where we are combining all different genre of design: post modernism, traditional English, Art Deco, minimalism, retro-sixties and Scandinavian. The result is really eclectic.'

Previous page and this page: vintage Reeves subtlety. He mixes checks and stripes as effortlessly as he does elements from different eras. He always installs "the most comfortable bed your budget can stand".

'What is gripping about interior design at the moment is that we are going through a general transition period. Three or four years ago, what was called minimalism is now mainstream. People understand what minimalism can be now.'

Reeves' mastery of texture is obvious in his own Fulham Road showroom, where he has just launched his first furniture collection.

'You have to constantly edit to get a distillation of all the good in each of the looks. We have gone through a patch of extreme masculinity in interior design and we are now bringing in a bit of femininity – not floral stuff, just lush and pretty elements. The harmony comes when you have the best of the masculine mixed with the best of the feminine.'

M arc Hertrich

Designer: Marc Hertrich. **Country:** France. **Style:** Mixing a lot of colour with the old and new. **Work:** About ten projects at a time

including restaurants, hotels and private houses and apartments. **Favourite colour:** I use a lot of blue but never on its own - I always mix colours. **Vital element:** Lighting, as it creates magic and charm. Without it you can destroy the space. **Must have:** Comfort, such as large sofas. **Object of desire:** A tree house or even a house that is built in the air. **Most inspiring buildings:** The Guggenheim in Bilbao and the crazy buildings that are mixed up together in Hong Kong. I also love the temples in Thailand. **Admired designers:** There are many such as Philippe Starck and Arne Jacobsen. **Good shopping:** Foreign markets that you come across while travelling and, for general shopping, it must be London, Paris and New York. **Best buy:** A big metal toy Ferris wheel that no one really knows anything about - it could be 19th century. **Pet hates:** Design for the sake of it.

Hertrich always mixes colour in his schemes and emphasises lighting to create magic and charm.

'When I design a public space, I like to create an "event". That way people can dream in our places. It is the same for the design of a house, just more subtle.'

Stephen Falcke

Designer: Stephen Falcke. **Country:** South Africa. **Style:** Not to have a particular style and to create simple comfortable rooms. **Work:** Mainly residential projects - up to 30 at a time - in South Africa, Australia, London and France. **Favourite colours:** I love using no colour at all such as white on white or to break the rules and use strong colour and have all tones of green together or all tones of blue. **Vital element:** Proportion. I love 'undecorated' shapely rooms. **Must have:** Comfort. To be able to sit easily and read easily. **Object of desire:** An Egyptian chair that I once saw, but could not afford. It had the most wonderful proportions and hoofed legs. **Most inspiring building:** The Taj Mahal. It has true mystique. **Admired designers:** John Stefanidis. His work has a wonderful easiness on the eye. David Mlinaric is incredible for his knowledge and historical eye. **Good shopping:** London, as I relate to English things better than anything else. **Best buy:** A pair of silver candlesticks that I bought at Sotheby's about five years ago. They are the most simple, beautiful things and are worth about four times what I paid. **Pet hate:** Over-decorated or over-lit rooms.

Simple, comfortable rooms created for a bachelor.

A quirky mix of colonial, African and French influences at The Garden House.

'An interior should complement the person who lives there. It is just like creating the right stage for the right actor.'

'There should always be
something amusing in a room,
something that is out of context

and makes you laugh. It could be
a wonderful naive child's painting
that is hung in a grand space.'

Kelly Hoppen Interiors

Designer: Kelly Hoppen. **Country:** United Kingdom. **Style:** Creating individual homes - nobody wants to have the same as the next person any more. **Work:** Up to 30 residential and commercial projects at any one time. **Favourite colours:** Definitely taupe, but I also love purple, which, I am told, can become addictive. **Vital element:** Music piped throughout the entire house is essential. **Must have:** A cappuccino machine and a place to reflect. **Object of desire:** My bath. It is the most heavenly place in the entire world. **Most inspiring buildings:** Both the V&A and the British Museum are

incredibly inspiring as they are so packed with wonderful things. **Admired designers:** Christian Liaigre and Philippe Starck are very clever designers and I would put Le Corbusier and Richard Rogers at the top of my list for architects. **Good shopping:** Frankly, anywhere. Any city. I love shopping in Paris and Milan and obviously in the Far East. **Best buy:** Two chairs that I spotted in a Paris market that are made in stainless steel with suede lilac upholstery. They are absolutely perfect. **Pet hates:** Chintz, festoon blinds, Austrian curtains, and net curtains. Chocolate brown and orange together are awful and so are brown and blue together, but brown, blue and gold are even worse.

'If you feel comfortable in your own home then other people will too - so much so that they do not wish to leave.'

'The East meets West approach is still very much a part of my work, but the look has evolved and is more about the feeling of that look. Harmony, style and

simplicity – that's essentially what the Kelly Hoppen look is about now. Above all else, everything has to feel right and to be comfortable and calm.'

Howard Wiggins

Designer: Howard Wiggins. **Country:** United States. **Style:** Determining the line between too much and too little. I like my rooms to look as though they have evolved over a long period of time. **Work:** Mainly residential, with at least 20 projects in progress at a time. **Favourite colours:** I like all colours, particularly black and coral, but I would never shy away from any colour. **Vital element:** Atmosphere and comfort. **Must have:** A sense of the unexpected - I may put a picture on the floor behind the piano or place a sterling silver spider on the wall. **Object of desire:** Art and sculpture. **Most inspiring building:** The Chrysler Building in New York. It has a romantic feel that evokes a period in time when contemporary style was the vogue - just as it is now. **Admired designer:** The Dallas designer, Lloyd Paxton. He has a clean-cut approach to design that I love. **Good shopping:** I find treasures wherever I go, but Nashville has pretty good shopping. **Best buy:** My 400-year-old wooden bed that is inlaid with ivory, teak and rosewood. It is now worth a fortune. **Pet hates:** Poor workmanship and bad materials.

'Colour is coming in with a vengeance. We have had 20 years of neutrals and now it is time for colour.'

Tara Bernerd

Designer: Tara Bernerd. **Country:** United Kingdom. **Style:** Contemporary style that does not date because I use very natural materials. **Work:** Development of one property at a time. **Favourite colour:** That is impossible to answer. **Vital element:** Good natural light and flexible lighting. **Must have:** A good kitchen and, if possible, it should have true daylight. **Object of desire:** Knockout contemporary art. **Most inspiring buildings:** I.M. Pei's Four Seasons Hotel in New York and there is a hotel that is out of this world in Ubud, Bali. It is contemporary but is right in the middle of the jungle. I love that. **Admired designer:** I adore the work of the Argentinean architect, the late Louis Barragan, and I also admire the builders in Indonesia who make ordinary houses from bamboo. **Good shopping:** You can find treasures in most capitals, but I always head for the back streets of Amsterdam for a little Buddha, to Balinese villages for beaded tassels and to Marrakech for lanterns. **Best buy:** A Japanese chest that I bought on the King's Road in London that sits at the end of my bed. **Pet hates:** Too much green and salmon pink, hideous sofas, the wrong colour of stone and nasty china pots.

'I love the feeling of concrete walls. If you added tan leather, it would suddenly create both a colour and a feeling.'

Anika Reuterswärd

Designer: Anika Reuterswärd. **Country:** Sweden. **Style:** Modern, with soul - that means very clean and light, but at the same time warm and homely. **Work:** Both commercial and residential projects, plus journalism, interior styling and furniture design. **Favourite colours:** White. And white, black and Chinese Red together. You never tire of that combination. **Vital element:** Daylight and how the light comes into the room. **Must have:** A big table, because that is where you do everything. Eat, chat, gather, everything. **Object of desire:** A perfect English style garden with a gardener. **Most inspiring building:** The Guggenheim in Bilbao. It is like nothing else in the world. **Admired designer:** Sir Terence Conran. He is my guru, because his approach is so functional, while at the same time being so expressive. **Good shopping:** Garden centres in the South of France. **Best buy:** I never strike bargains, but there is a drawing that I bought from a fashion illustrator, Mats Gustavson, of a naked woman and it is absolutely marvellous. **Pet hate:** Hiding windows with a lot of fabric. I never over furnish - always go for the less is more approach.

A stunning weekend retreat in the Archipelago of Stockholm, Anika Reuterswärd has intentionally left the finish casual.

'Minimalism means that there should be a very few simple things – simple furniture, simple details. What comes after minimalism is sensualism. This is a softening of minimalism and much greater comfort.'

Reuterswärd never over furnishes a scheme – she always opts for a 'less is more' approach.

Rustic charm meets French chic at a village house in Provence. Overleaf: Reuterswärd uses white on white and white and black as a classic combination.

Future Classics

Designer: Heidi Arenstein. **Country:** South Africa. **Style:** Contemporary, with a strong African flavour. **Work:** Mainly residential with some commercial jobs, plus bespoke furniture commissions. Generally there are two large projects and 30 smaller jobs in progress. **Favourite colour:** White, because it is so easy to live with.

Vital element: Liveability. A space has to be easy to live in. **Must have:** Space. **Object of desire:** A black swimming pool. **Most inspiring building:** The Arcadia, which is a Jewish orphanage in Johannesburg. It was designed by Herbert Baker and is a beautiful, though run-down, classical building with the most unbelievable proportions. It has the sort of scale you simply don't get in new buildings. **Admired designer:** My mother, Ruth Lipschitz, as her work is both practical and beautiful. She is a real inspiration. **Good shopping:** Milan would be my first choice and London my second. **Best buy:** A Judith Mason drawing - I bought it before I had a home of my own when I was 19. I just had to have it, as it is a very simple abstract line drawing of a hand. **Pet hate:** I hate spaces that are over-decorated with too much matching.

Arenstein's gift for furniture design and soft interiors is marked by an African influence.

'Design is going back to basics. For so long there has been the perception that the more you have the better it is, however that is changing and there is a definite trend for paring down.'

Gluckstein Design

Designer: Brian Gluckstein. **Country:** Canada. **Style:** A look that is eclectic and incorporates strong architectural detailing. **Work:** Both residential and hospitality - one third of the projects are country clubs in Canada - and there are generally between 50 and 70 in progress including the most famous, Glen Abbey. **Favourite colours:** Neutral palettes. **Vital element:** The management and co-ordination of the project. That is what makes it successful.

Must have: A two-storey library - there is never enough room for books. **Object of desire:** A palazzo in Venice. **Most inspiring building:** I like the way I.M.Pei's glass pyramid at the Louvre in Paris complements the historic site. **Admired designers:** One of my favourites is New York's John Saladino. Christian Liaigre's work has a cleanness and purity that is very refreshing and I also admire the late Jean Michel Frank for his chic, timeless, thirties interior design. **Good shopping:** New York for variety and Toronto for world-class antiques and silver. **Best buy:** Two Charles Rennie Mackintosh chairs that I bought when I was in my early twenties. **Pet hates:** Gaudiness - and rooms that are uncomfortable, no matter how beautiful.

Gluckstein uses neutral palettes to create the right background for art and antique collections.

'I like to put pieces of furniture, carpets and art together so that the finished look reflects different cultures and periods.'

John Minshaw Designs

Designer: John Minshaw. **Country:** United Kingdom. **Style:** Bespoke interiors that are dramatic but enticingly empty. **Work:** About three large houses each year. **Favourite colour:** I have always loved blue, as it is an infinite colour. **Vital element:** Light. If that is not right then nothing else looks right. **Must have:** One of those pump-action pencils - I work with them all the time. **Object of desire:** A Gulwing Mercedes as it is like the most marvellous piece of sculpture. **Most inspiring buildings:** The Egyptian pyramids. They are fabulous self-supporting structures and the higher up the pyramid you go the less building materials you need. Incredible. **Admired designer:** The late Nicholas Hawksmoor. He made working within the constraints of classicism uniquely his. You just have to look at his buildings in Spittalfields and St George's in the Fields in London to see why. **Good shopping:** Paris is best as it still has small independent and interesting specialist shops. **Best buy:** A small six by four-inch pen and ink drawing of three Egyptian columns. I paid £1 for it in a Greenwich market when I was a student. **Pet hates:** Chintz and over-complicated things.

'What I do is evolutionary rather than revolutionary.'

Minshaw excels at creating restrained, dramatic, classical rooms as shown in this London house.

'Everything we do is bespoke. I even design all the fittings, furniture and joinery. It's become my trademark.'

The foyer, bar and restaurant at One Aldwych, in London.

Fox Linton Associates

Designer: Mary Fox Linton. **Country:** United Kingdom. **Style:** Contemporary and elegant, with a mix of old and new. **Work:** Between four and six, large, mainly residential projects at a time. **Favourite colours:** Neutrals with shots of colour. **Vital element:** Use of space because space and light are a luxury, especially in a city. **Must haves:** A power shower, white plates, a dishwasher and a small tape

measure that fits into my handbag. **Object of desire:** A rock crystal Mogul bowl at the V&A Museum. The design is so simple that it could have been made today. **Most inspiring building:** The Chrysler Building in New York. It never ceases to please me every time I see it. **Admired designers:** The architect, the late Louis Barragan, and the architect, Paolo Tommasi, who is streets ahead of his time. **Good shopping:** Italy. I like what the Italians make and I like their finish. **Best buy:** A Mirror Black Chinese brush pot that I bought at auction in a lot, along with an ironing board and an electric fire. The total cost was 50p. **Pet hates:** Coloured baths and washbasins, floral wallpaper borders and short curtains and gold taps.

Fox Linton gutted the interior of the old Morning Post newspaper building to create the stunning modern spaces at One Aldwych. Below, The Axis Restaurant.

The bronze bust by Andre Wallace in the foyer of One Aldwych is almost Stalinist in its proportions.

'Obviously design will become more technological, but it must also be comfortable.'

'You are always innovating when you are an interior designer. You never do the same thing twice, which is thrilling.'

The health club at One Aldwych and overleaf a glass house conversion in London.

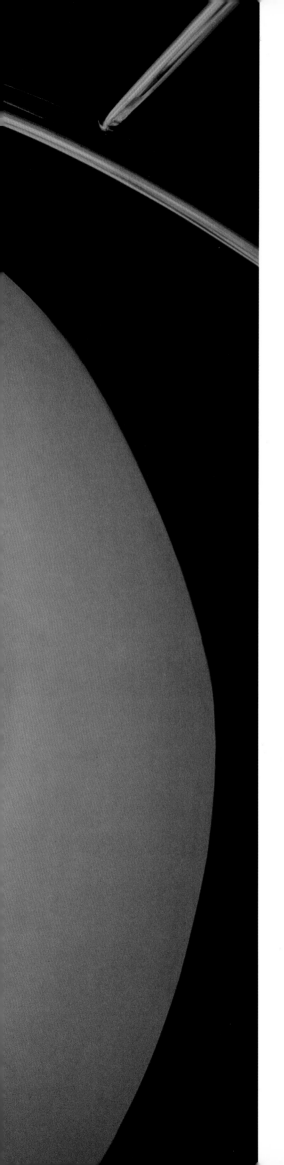

Etchika Werner

Designer: Etchika Werner. **Country:** Germany. **Style:** A classic but not old-fashioned look with a witty mix of things that should not really go together, but do. **Work:** Both residential and commercial, with up to ten jobs at

a time. **Favourite colours:** Red and very strong green, but, of course, blue and white are very beautiful too. **Vital element:** Lighting - it creates the atmosphere. **Must have:** Good beds. I specialise in the design of good beds. **Object of desire:** A house built by the eighteenth century classical designer, Karl Frederich Shinkel. **Most inspiring building:** The Guggenheim museum in Bilbao - it is about the future. **Admired designers:** Anouska Hempel and I am also impressed by Zandra Rhodes. **Good shopping:** I rarely shop, but I love London for the houses and architecture. **Best buy:** The most beautiful thing I have bought is a dress by Zandra Rhodes. It is 20 years old and I treat it as a museum piece. **Pet hate:** Bad workmanship.

'The first thing I ask clients is what colours they like. From that I can more or less tell what style they want.'

'The beds I design are based on antique beds – they are full of fabric, perhaps have a canopy, but always have lots of cushions in fabulous fabrics. However, a very good mattress comes first.'

Anita Brooks & Associates

Designers: Anita Brooks, Charles Gruwell. **Country:** United States. **Style:** Elegant, comfortable design. **Work:** Hospitality projects such as the Animal Kingdom Lodge for Disney in Florida. Between eight and ten hotels and about five private houses are under construction at any one time. **Favourite colour:** Cinnamon - it's a mixture of red and brown and creates an earthy elegance. **Vital element:** The architectural 'envelope'. **Must have:** That a space should be comfortable and relaxing. **Object of desire:** A home overlooking the river in Ubud, Bali. **Most inspiring buildings:** Italianate Paladian architecture inspires me tremendously, as does the work of the 16th century architect, Palladio. **Admired designer:** The best in the world was the late James Northcutt. He designed some of the most exclusive and elegant hotels. **Good shopping:** Italy for classical objects, beautiful paintings, carvings and gilt mirrors and Bali for the natural and uncontrived artefacts. I love to mix the two together. **Best buy:** Unbelievable Indonesian tables made from old, old wood which are to the right scale and cost a fraction of what they would anywhere else in the world. **Pet hates:** Blue interiors and ultra stark minimal spaces.

'Blank minimalism does nothing for me. I am into texture and artefacts and layers of natural fabrics and objects.'

79

Heiberg Cummings Design

Designers: Bernt Heiberg, William Cummings. **Country:** Norway. **Style:** Scandinavian modernism, done in a way that works for now. **Work:** 80 percent residential with up to five projects split between the Oslo and New York offices. **Favourite colour:** I don't have a favourite colour but white is invaluable as it does not interrupt anything. **Vital element:** The application of light - both natural and artificial. **Must have:** A comfortable sofa. **Object of desire:** A nice holiday in Greece. **Most inspiring building:** The Flat Iron Building in New York. It's like a slither that sits on the cross-section of Fifth Avenue and Broadway. **Admired designers:** Michael Graves, the post-modern American architect. I also admire Sir Terence Conran for his way of collecting objects into a style. **Good shopping:** Stockholm for antiques as there is an enormous wealth of objects and, of course, New York is fantastic for everything. **Best buy:** My wooden workers cottage in Oslo. It's where my partner, Bernt Heiberg, and I started this business. The design of that house was the genesis of everything that we are doing now. **Pet hate:** It makes me crazy when people ask your opinion about design but are not interested in hearing your answer.

'I tend to be the concept builder and my partner, Bernt Heiberg, is very good at finishing and details.'

'We are at a big transition point – people have taken modernism as far as it can go, which is

why I use the term post-modernism to describe what the trend has been for the past few years.'

Roof top view of Beijing's China Club.

The Architectural Practice

Designers: Patrick Kwan, Hamish Cowperthwaite, Kelvin Au. **Country:** Hong Kong.

Style: Traditional, old-fashioned, colonial style projects - I enjoy that kind of work the most. **Work:** Up to 15 projects at a time, including hotels, clubs, bars and restaurants in Hong Kong, China, Kathmandu and Delhi. **Favourite colours:** Cream

and dark green, plus strong natural colours. **Vital element:** That the client has an adequate budget to achieve what he wants to see at the end of the day. **Must have:** A good bathroom. **Object of desire:** A distant view, preferably of the sea. **Most inspiring buildings:** The Forbidden City in Beijing - but I also like Brown's Hotel in London, I.M. Pei's pyramid at the Louvre in Paris and the Bank of China Tower in Hong Kong. **Admired designer:** Charles Rennie Mackintosh - his designs are very interesting. **Good shopping:** One of the computer malls in Hong Kong and I love the cheese and clothes shops in Jermyn Street, London. **Best buy:** My desk. It's a Ming painting table, which means it is rather high. **Pet hates:** Bad workmanship, a poorly assembled building and bad planning.

'The quality of design coming out of Hong Kong is improving all the time. Clients on the whole are better educated and are able to differentiate between good design and poor design.'

Most of Cowperthwaite's work is huge commercial projects in Hong Kong, China and Burma.

'The master bathroom must be beautiful so that you enjoy being in it. It should be large, have a good-sized vanity counter, a decent sized bath, and, a loo in a separate compartment.'

'My Russian clients want their homes to be as Western as possible because they see everything from their past as being basic and backward. They want that real cutting edge feeling.'

A.J.B Interiors

Designer: Angie Diggle. **Country:** Russia. **Style:** Taking a space and making the best of it. I prefer traditional furnishing, but at the same time, I like to pare that look down so that it isn't too heavy or fussy. **Work:** Residential projects, all of which are based in Moscow. **Favourite colours:** I tend toward natural colours, but I am also drawn to warm colours like burgundy and deep orange. **Vital element:**

Order. **Must have:** A measuring tape. **Object of desire:** A beautiful piece of modern furniture that had not been seen before. **Most inspiring building:** The Ministry of Defence in Moscow - the proportions are wonderfully over-exaggerated. **Admired designer:** The Art Deco architect, Schetel. **Good shopping:** I am a lighting fiend, so it would have to be Besselink & Jones, but I also get a bit 'goose-bumpy' when I visit Percheron as their silks are fantastic. **Best buy:** A ton of Ikea furniture that I shipped to Moscow. I painted it and added press-studs and other details and it just looks great. Such a bargain. **Pet hates:** Working with builders who tell me what to do - Russian builders are very good at having their own opinions.

Reed Creative

Designer: Jonathan Reed. **Country:** United Kingdom. **Style:** A strong architectural approach with the emphasis on materials and texture, line and form. **Work:** Mainly large residential projects in Europe and America. **Favourite**

colours: The colours of the moors, such as greys, greens and soft purples. **Vital element:** A sense of scale. Even in a small space, scale creates visual impact. **Must have:** Focus. That could be a material like wood or stone or a reference to a piece of furniture or architectural detail. **Object of desire:** Time. **Most inspiring building:** The Chapel of the Holy Cross in Sedona, Arizona. It was built in 1952 and is an awe-inspiring, modern building that is totally integrated into its natural surroundings. **Admired designer:** Sir Edwin Lutyens. He was an architect and true interior designer who gave as much attention to the practical working of an interior as he did to the exterior. **Good shopping:** Los Angeles. There is a certain frivolity to the place and it is full of things that were created by insane designers for insane clients. It is where you will find the

most incredible outdoor furniture and the most amazing mid-century furniture. **Best buy:** A huge lamp by Jean

Besnard that I bought when I was 18 and had no money. Now he is considered to be one of the most collected 20th century potters. **Pet hate:** Trends, such as the fashion for beige.

'Being able to turn off your partner's bedside light from your side of the bed is one of the most important things in a bedroom.'

Zeynep Fadillioglu

Designer: Zeynep Fadillioglu. **Country:** Turkey. **Style:** Creating a warm atmosphere by putting old and new together. **Work:** Restaurants, clubs and houses - a maximum of eight each year. **Favourite colours:** Burgundy and green - all aged of course. **Vital element:** Timeless decoration. I don't like things that look just 'so 1999'. **Must have:** A house with a lived-in, happy spirit. **Object of desire:** An incredible floor cushion - I sit on the floor all the time. **Most inspiring building:** The Glasshouse at the Louvre in Paris. The structure is very exciting as it symbolises contemporary design. It brings a different edge to an old building. **Admired designer:** Philippe Starck. There is a lot of wit in his work even though much of it looks so plain. **Good shopping:** There is a fabulous shop in the covered bazaar in Istanbul that sells beautiful Anatolian textiles, but I also love shopping in Dehli, Bombay and Bangkok. **Best buy:** An Ottoman vase that I bought for less than $10 in a Bombay flea market. **Pet hates:** Anything that matches or that is fashion dictated - both these things are characterless and can become monotonous.

Fadillioglu's is a seamless blend of old and new with the emphasis on ottoman antiques.

'I find my 'spirit' through people who are young and contemporary in their outlook. Each time I work on a project there are different people contributing. I do not believe in 'I', I believe in 'We'.'

'A place has to be fresh, to feel fresh. Lighting is extremely important, colour is important, finish is important.'

These richly decorated interiors rely on scale and simple styling.

Emanuel Gomes

Designer: Emanuel Gomes. **Country:** Portugal. **Style:** I am a bit of a chameleon as I change 'colour' to suit the client. **Work:** Consulates, embassies and other government buildings, plus apartments and houses - generally one large project and a few smaller jobs at a time. **Favourite colours:** Whatever colours are suitable for the project become my favourites. **Vital element:** Lighting. **Must have:** Art that has been bought for pleasure. **Object of desire:** An English style conservatory where I could mix art and other objects with plants and trees. **Most inspiring building:** The new Guggenheim in Bilbao - it is adventurous and innovative and without doubt a piece of art. **Admired designer:** The Finnish architect, the late Alvar Aalto. He was a natural environmentalist with a very organic way of interpreting materials and space. **Good shopping:** I like John Hobbs the antique dealer in Pimlico, London, but I am also crazy about toys and always have to visit Hamleys whenever I am in London. **Best buy:** A painting by the Portuguese artist, Eduardo Batarda, that I bought last year. **Pet hates:** Cheap workmanship, clutter and an un-functional environment.

Alexandra Champalimaud & Associates

Designer: Alexandra Champalimaud. **Country:** United States. **Style:** Interiors that are well proportioned, pared down and very easy to live with. **Work:** About 15 projects at one time split between houses, hotels and restaurants in both North and South America. **Favourite colour:** I love red. I look good in it. I understand colour and use it with absolutely no reservation. **Vital element:** The space - its size, position and mood. **Must have:** A great view.

You need something in the distance to transport you. **Object of desire:** Heat, sunshine and being outdoors. And anything to do with the sea. **Most inspiring building:** The Shanghai Bank in Hong Kong. It looks magnificent and is orderly and tranquil in the middle of the chaos of the city. **Admired designer:** I.M.Pei. He is a modernist whose work is also very classic in its form and scale. **Good shopping:** London for lovely old fabrics and Portugal for fabulous old stones. **Best buy:** Some ancient embroidered Chinese skirts that I bought in a New York auction about two months ago. I think they are between 200 and 250 years old. **Pet hates:** Anything over-stuffed, a profusion of objects - I cannot stand that - and bad lighting.

'I often use white as it is the background to everything.'

The famous Algonquin Hotel in New York.
(Pages 114 - 117)

M.D.l.D

Designers: Malcolm Duffin, Paul Douglas. **Country:** United Kingdom. **Style:** Classicism that is eclectic, modern and contemporary. **Work:** Residential, with between 12 to 15 projects in progress. **Favourite colours:** I don't have a favourite colour, but blue comes close... I do however love using black and lacquer. **Vital element:** Cohesion. **Must have:** Visual dynamics - a sense of form and structure. **Object of desire:** Prints and paintings by Piranesi and Canaletto. **Most inspiring buildings:** The new Guggenheim museum in Bilbao - it is classic, linear and one of its kind. The new Royal Scottish Museum in Chambers Street, Edinburgh, is the most stunning building in Scotland. **Admired designer:** The late Billy Baldwin who was an American decorator in the fifties. **Good shopping:** Hermes in Paris, not for what you can buy, but because it is one of the most beautiful shops in the world. **Best buy:** A Piranesi print that I bought when I was a baby designer aged 20. **Pet hates:** Anything that looks offensively kitsch and expensive and amateur decoration with matching fabrics and borders.

'I like it when a client resists the temptation to conform. One of my favourite combinations is a set of French Louis XVI salon chairs round a glass and steel table.'

'I like symmetry. I am a slave to symmetry, but the look I most like is textured, uncluttered, simple and beautifully lit.'

'I wanted to bring new interior design to Scotland. I am trying to break the mould – it is a personal ambition.'

Joseph Sy & Associate

Designer: Joseph Sy. **Country:** Hong Kong. **Style:** Contemporary style. I like things to be clean and uncluttered. **Work:** About ten residential and commercial projects at a time - offices and high rise buildings in Manila and Hong Kong and projects in Jakarta and China. **Favourite colours:** Beige and off white, with some punches of dark colour. **Vital element:** Lighting. **Must have:** A hi-fi that delivers good sound. **Object of desire:** Music and art, but music is my priority. **Most inspiring building:** The glass pyramid at the Louvre in Paris. It is transparent and symbolic and makes a very strong statement. **Admired designers:** Philippe Starck for his surprising designs, and I also admire the architects, John Pawson, I.M. Pei and Frank Lloyd Wright. **Good shopping:** Rome is a lovely place to stroll around and Tokyo has great shopping - I am a better window shopper than a buyer. **Best buy:** A painting called Oranges 1993 that I bought three years ago. It is by Janet Stayton who paints with brilliant colour. **Pet hates:** Anything fussy with too many details, badly lit houses and complicated planning.

'When you look back over time, good classic design always comes back to simplicity.'

'A straightforward, simple plan is vital. It must be economically feasible and technically possible.'

Sy uses "punches of colour" to emphasise his clean-lined architecture and masterful lighting. In contrast he uses his favourite colour combination of beige and off white in the living spaces.
(Pages 124 - 125)

Ocampo-Tanferna

Designer: Laura Ocampo. **Country:** Argentina. **Style:** For things to 'meet', even though they are not perfectly 'matched'. **Work:** Both commercial and residential projects, mainly in Buenos Aires. **Favourite colours:** Grey white, beige white, dirty white . . . they make the best backgrounds to tobacco tones and combinations of reds. **Vital element:** Harmony between the space and what is in it. **Must have:** Comfort. **Object of desire:** Philippe Starck's sofa bed - it is timeless and has perfect proportion. **Most inspiring building:** Capella Pazzi in Florence. It looks very bare because of all the grey and white and its proportions are absolutely right. **Admired designer:** John Saladino. His work is classic. **Good shopping:** New York. It is inspiring and spontaneous and full of possibilities. **Best buy:** A strange little Victorian bed that is long and skinny, that I bought for a client. Argentinean paintings can also be very good buys. **Pet hates:** When rooms look too finished, too decorated or too perfect. Or when a home is so impersonal you get the feeling that nobody lives there.

'I like to be creative with what is to hand as you achieve a quality to the work that is totally unique and inventive.'

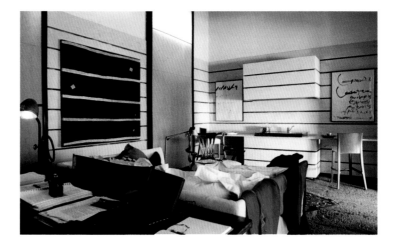

Wilson & Associates

Designers: Shiree Darley, Paul Duesing. **Country:** South Africa. **Style:** A mix of European and African, always taking the environment into consideration. **Work:** Hotels and leisure, plus luxury residential projects. **Favourite colour:** Washed ochre - it is a tone with a lot of depth to it. **Vital element:** Proportion and scale. **Must have:** Ambience.

Object of desire: A beautiful wildlife oil painting by Hannes du Plessis. It is of a leopard on a bank at sunset with a misty river in the background. **Most inspiring building:** The Izingwe Game Lodge in Welgevonden, South Africa. I love it because it is simple and elegant. **Admired designer:** The South African interior designer, Trisha Wilson. She has such a natural eye and so much style. **Good shopping:** The streets of Mexico and the local flea markets here. **Best buy:** A beautiful, carved, dark teak table with two stools that I spotted on a roadside stall. The wood is cracked and aged and each piece is in the shape of a woman. I loaded them into my boot on the spot. **Pet hate:** Curtains that are hung at the same height as the top of the window instead of at ceiling height. It kills the proportion of the room.

'You can have a room that has very little in it, but if the scale and proportion is true, then it will still look very special.'

'There is such a variety of cultures and traditions in South Africa. I have always taken references from culture and every project gives me the chance to bring in some of those different elements. It is very inspiring.'

The Zimbali Game Lodge is one of South Africa's finest.

'Less is more. We try to bring both intelligence and elegance into the spaces we design. We try to achieve a clean look and not use more materials than we have to.'

Ahlsén & Tengbom

Designers: Erik Ahlsén, Nilla Cronstedt. **Country:** Sweden. **Style:** A Scandinavian-modern look inspired by both high-tech and English styles. **Work:** A mix of work with about 15 projects in progress. **Favourite colours:** Blues and greens are good colours in Nordic light. They are very cheering and make you feel relaxed. **Vital element:** The air and light must be right for the building. **Must have:** Dogs. They make your life very rich. **Object of desire:** Order. **Most inspiring building:** Lloyd's of London is my personal favourite - it is a surprise when you see it. The design is so intelligent.

Admired designer: The Finnish architect, the late Alvar Aalto. His buildings are very exact and strict - and he managed to bring light right into them, making them shimmer. **Good shopping:** Window shopping in the beautiful streets in both Italy and Florence. **Best buy:** Two years ago, I bought an old brewery that I am re-designing and turning into a summerhouse. **Pet hates:** Small ugly things you put on tables everywhere and I also dislike ugly or over-decorated restaurants.

Christian de Falbe

Designer: Christian de Falbe. **Country:** United Kingdom. **Style:** To take things from different periods and jumble them up a bit, so you end up with something that does not necessarily follow the rules. **Work:** Residential and some restaurants - a maximum of 12 jobs a year. **Favourite colours:** Any colour that is on the cusp or dividing line between two colours. For instance, I love the colour between purple and blue. **Vital element:** Atmosphere -

the feeling of being welcome when you walk in the front door. **Must have:** A bath that is big enough and fills up quickly with hot soapy water. **Object of desire:** Flowers with a pool of light on them - that always looks gorgeous. **Most inspiring building:** The Villa Guilia in Rome. Classical architecture makes me draw in my breath. **Admired designers:** The sixteenth century architect, Palladio, but I'm also a great admirer of Christoph Gollut and Alidad. **Good shopping:** Secret architectural salvage places. I love to find a bargain. **Best buy:** A pair of immaculate black marble spheres that I bid for at the Bunny Roger auction about a year ago. **Pet hates:** Things that match and coloured towels and bedlinen - they must be white.

'Diplomacy, charm and patience are vital components of this job.'

'I like all materials to have a built in patina – paint work should be faded or chalky, wood should be worn, waxed, bleached or grainy, velvet has to be crunchy. These things have to be sensual and interesting to touch.'

De Falbe is as happy working with traditional furnishing as he is with contemporary – providing he can "jumble them up".

Jane Churchill Interiors

Designer: Jane Churchill. **Country:** United Kingdom. **Style:** Traditional interiors with a witty contemporary twist. **Work:** Both residential and commercial projects - between 10 and 15 at a time - in Australia, Barbados, Finland, London and Ireland. **Favourite colour:** I am a blue person, but I always put red into blue paints so that the blue is not too cold. **Vital element:** Comfort with a capital C. **Must have:** Comfortable beds and comfortable sofas. **Object of desire:** I have a penchant for candles and candelabra. Candlelight is so pretty, particularly if the candles are reflected in mirrors. **Most inspiring building:** My Aunt Nancy's (Lancaster) house. It inspired me the most as it was grand, but it oozed comfort and it did not have fake poshness. **Admired designer:** The late Nancy Lancaster. **Good shopping:** My own shop. **Best buy:** The oval gilt mirror in my bedroom - it has been in every one of my houses. **Pet hates:** I loathe navy blue in decorating, as it is too hard. I also dislike badly made or short curtains, but at the same time, I don't like curtains that fall into 'puddles' on the floor.

'Gilt looks good with everything, whether it is put with white or a floral background.'

'Chucking money at decoration is not the answer. Either you have style and taste or you don't.'

Mark Simmons Interiors

Designer: Mark Simmons. **Country:** United States. **Style:** Clean, classical style with lots of old objects. **Work:** Mainly residential with up to 25 projects in progress. **Favourite colour:** An aged terracotta red - it gives a lot of punch to a room. **Vital element:** The furniture arrangement must be workable and have 'flow'. **Must have:** Lamps and good lighting. **Object of desire:** Good art, as it can make or break a room. **Most inspiring buildings:** Blenheim Palace, England, and The Mansion Hotel in Turtle Creek, Dallas. I like the old-world ambience of both places. Blakes is my favourite hotel in London. **Admired designer:** The late Mark Hampton, who was a New York-based interior designer. He created very elegant interiors. **Good shopping:** London's Portobello Road market - it's one of the most fun places to shop in the world. **Best buy:** An oil painting by an unnamed artist that I picked up in an American market. I really enjoy looking at it. **Pet hates:** Itty-bitty accessories and things that are out of proportion to the rest of the room. And I despise skimpy curtains.

'A few really good objects and pieces of furniture are better than lots of lesser things.'

'I like my houses to have a warmth and glow – an inviting feeling and I despise skimpy curtains'

Mark Simmons' southern American style mixes classical lines with lots of objects, although he dislikes 'itty-bitty' objects.

Terence Disdale Design

Designer: Terence Disdale. **Country:** United Kingdom. **Style:** A look that appears to have happened rather than one that looks as though it has been 'done'. **Work:** Up to nine super-yachts under construction at a time.

Favourite colours: Ivory and mint green, coral and turquoise. **Vital element:** Space planning. How you get from A to B, particularly the service passageways for crew. This makes or breaks a good yacht. **Must have:** On super-yachts, it must be windows. The whole style and layout of the room revolves around them. **Object of desire:** More time off work to go fishing in India. **Most inspiring buildings:** New York's Guggenheim Museum - it is brilliant.

I also like the M15 head quarters as it is one of the better modern buildings in London. **Admired designer:** The late Buckminster Fuller. He was a total genius and such a revolutionary designer, whether he was working on cars, geodesic domes or his incredible buildings. **Good shopping:** Andrew Martin (I must be their best customer), Albrissi has a wonderful selection of objects and Yeoward South has great furniture and accessories. **Best buy:** A pair of stunning Burmese temple doors that I bought in Bangkok about 15 years ago. They were a real gift. **Pet hates:** Man-made fibres and over-varnished wood.

'A boat should look like a boat. Why should it look like a Manhattan apartment?'

'People are becoming much more tuned to the fact that you don't have to take your gold taps and crystal chandeliers on board.'

Disdale's ground-breaking super yacht interiors; nothing like this has been done before.

'Space planning comes first. It is easy to decorate a room and make it look good, but it would be a hopeless design if the steward has to walk through it with a load of laundry to get from one part of the yacht to another.'

João Mansur

Designer: João Mansur. **Country:** Brazil. **Style:** Geometrical, symmetrical and classic with a modern touch. **Work:** Up to 15 large projects at a time, including restaurants and private homes. **Favourite colours:** Brown, black and dark green mixed with red. **Vital element:** The right lighting, which gives a space its mood. **Must have:** Diet Coke and retail therapy. **Object of desire:** A piece of furniture by Jacob Freres, a pied a terre close to the Seine in

Paris and a 1955 convertible Mercedes. **Most inspiring buildings:** The perfect symmetry created by the buildings in the Place de Vendome in Paris. **Admired designers:** The Brazilian landscape designer and architect, Roberto Burle-Max and the German architect and furniture designer, the late Mies van der Rohe, who created visionary, futuristic buildings. **Good shopping:** No real favourite places - I prefer to discover shopping in all cities. **Best buy:** An eighteenth century, eight leaf, Coromandel screen - I bought it from an estate sale when I was 22 knowing it was a good piece. I have since discovered that it came from one of the Chinese palaces and is worth a fortune. **Pet hate:** Characterless reproduction of antiques.

Insight West

Designers: Wayne Williamson, Sam Cardella, Bruce Goers. **Country:** United States. **Style:** Creating a comfortable space that makes you want to throw off your shoes and put your feet up. **Work:** Ten or so works in progress, including restaurants, commercial and residential projects. **Favourite colours:** Any and all colours. **Vital element:** To make the client satisfied beyond their expectations. **Must have:** Landscape - I use the surrounding landscape as my starting point. The exterior is an integral part of the interior. **Object of desire:** Fabulous bedlinen - there is nothing like it. **Most inspiring building:** There are so many inspiring buildings, but Frank Lloyd Wright's Falling Water is one of the most beautiful environments - both the architecture and the landscape. **Admired designers:** The architect, Frank Lloyd Wright, and the sculptor and painter, Samuel Botero. **Good shopping:** I shop everywhere - from Bangkok to second hand and garage sales. As they say 'one man's junk can be another man's treasure'. **Best buy:** All types of treasures from second hand and garage sales. **Pet hate:** Clutter.

'I love colour and love to use it. I am working on my own house at the moment and there are 38 colours.'

'I have a tremendous passion and energy for my work. I live, eat, breathe and

sleep it, in fact my whole life revolves around it.'

Cardella's chic but calming outdoor areas, plus a steam room in Rancho Mirage, California.

'Interior design is ever evolving just like fashion. We repeat history in everything we do.'

'There is no reason why there should be a dividing line between commercial and residential space. A commercial one should be as warm as a residential one – that cocoon feeling is what we all gravitate toward.'

Horne International

Designer: Charles Larry Horne. **Country:** United States. **Style:** I am a traditionalist who is fascinated by different cultures. **Work:** Residential projects in London, Kuwait, Saudi Arabia and America, with some commercial commissions - usually between ten and 15 projects of varying sizes at one time. **Favourite colours:** Classical colours. **Vital element:** Comfort. **Must have:** A sun room or conservatory - a room that brings the inside and outside together. **Object of desire:** Any kind of garden bench - I already have seven in my yard, all in different styles. **Most inspiring building:** Monticello, the home of Thomas Jefferson - he designed this house and was involved in every aspect of it. **Admired designers:** The late David Hicks for interior design and Robert Adam for architecture. **Good shopping:** John Rosselli in New York - many items are made by Rosselli - but there are also things for the garden, plus lots of antiques for sale. **Best buy:** My 1870s house in Fredericksburg, Virginia. It was dilapidated when I bought it in 1979 and has been an on-going project ever since. **Pet hate:** All-white rooms.

'I think of myself as having my feet in the twentieth century and my head in the twenty-first.'

'I am a classicist and love classical design in every culture. I am not creating museum rooms, but rooms that are comfortable to be in. They have the beauty of the past in a modern setting.'

'My interest is in colour and texture and all kinds of cultural weavings and carvings. I like to incorporate these things into whatever is appropriate for the job.'

A tented room in a Saudi Arabian palace.

173

Alison Henry Design

Designer: Alison Henry. **Country:** Hong Kong. **Style:** Dramatic and strong design that plays on contrasts and textures. **Work:** Restaurants and hotels, plus some residential work - about ten jobs at a time including a yacht and the Celine boutiques in Asia. **Favourite colours:** I always use white and black, as they are dramatic and create interesting effects. **Vital element:** Operational planning so there is no cross of traffic. **Must have:** The right consultants doing the right jobs. If you get the project right from the beginning, it saves a lot of money and time in the long run. **Object of desire:** To have my own design house where I could design anything I liked. **Most inspiring buildings:** I.M.Pei's Bank of China building and I also like the Chrysler building in New York. **Admired designer:** There are many, but I like what Anouska Hempel has created at both Blakes hotel and at The Hempel. **Good shopping:** The markets in northern Thailand for crafts such as tapestry, fabric panels, glass and silver. **Best buy:** Polished mother-of-pearl dishes that I bought for next to nothing on a beach in Thailand. **Pet hates:** Over-designed, fussy interiors.

'We went through the phase of everything being very clean and hard-edged, but we are moving toward a richer, more opulent look.'

175

'When you walk into
a room there should
be a focal point in
whatever direction
you look. It means

that you will not be distracted by everything else that is going on in the room.'

The opulent Garden Apartment at The Peninsula Hotel and the new Vong restaurant in The Mandarin Oriental - Hong Kong.

Todhunter Earle

Designers: Emily Todhunter, Kate Earle. **Country:** United Kingdom. **Style:** Creating an unpretentious, homey atmosphere. A house should feel happy, as though it has been like that forever. **Work:** Restaurants, hotels and large residential projects - up to 20 at a time. **Favourite colours:** Brown, beige, cream - I think that anything set against brown looks good. **Vital element:** The right lighting. You can have the nicest things in a house, but they will never look their best in bad lighting. **Must have:** Plain, simple combinations. **Object of desire:** A really special contemporary painting - one by Ivan Hitchins or Ben Nicholson. **Most inspiring building:** A palazzo in Florence called Rucellae, which is timeless, ancient and simply wonderful. **Admired designer:** The thirties designer, Jean Michel Frank. He was modern before modern became too over-the-top. His work was very, very chic. **Good shopping:** Open markets, bazaars and car boot sales - I think I am a born-again gypsy. And the shop, Valerie Wade, in London. **Best buy:** A grey upholstered chair that I bought five years ago from the thirties dealer, Gordon Watson. **Pet hates:** People with pet hates about decorating. Other than that, it could only be fringed tablecloths.

Le Manoir Aux Quat' Saisons where Emily Todhunter and her partner, Kate Earle, transformed what was a traditional country interior.

'The epitome of the look I love is what I call the contemporary classic: it is traditional without being too traditional and modern without being too modern.'

Grant White

Designer: Grant White. **Country:** United Kingdom. **Style:** Being a maximalist instead of a minimalist. I hate to do things by halves in either a traditional or contemporary interior. **Work:** Mainly residential with some commercial. Up to six large jobs at a time. **Favourite colours:** Aubergine is my all time favourite and reds. You can mix an enormous range of reds together and they look fabulous. **Vital element:** Understanding exactly what the client

wants. **Must have:** Cashmere everywhere. **Object of desire:** An amazing piece of Roman sculpture. **Most inspiring building:** The Desert de Retz. It's an amazing folly outside Paris that looks as if it were built as the most enormous base for a giant classical column. **Admired designer:** The late Renzo Mongiardino. His attention to detail was incredible. **Good shopping:** The markets and all the specialist shops in Paris. **Best buy:** A pair of forties console tables that I bought from Gallery 25 in London. I would never sell them. **Pet hates:** Primary colours and picture rails. They wreck the proportions of a room.

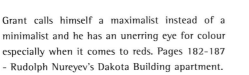

Grant calls himself a maximalist instead of a minimalist and he has an unerring eye for colour especially when it comes to reds. Pages 182-187 - Rudolph Nureyev's Dakota Building apartment.

'If rooms are large, it is much better to push the design as far as it can go rather than underplay it.'

'I love to play on the architecture of a room, it is the most important aspect of any space.'

The existing paneling in this hallway was repolished "to bring it back to life and give the space grandeur and proportion".

Played down English style in a variety of different projects.

'What is exciting at the moment is the whole appreciation for thirties, forties and fifties design.'

CONTENTS & DIRECTORY OF DESIGNERS